THE LIFE ASSIGNMENT

MW00991569

Praise for *The Life Assignment*

"The poems in *The Life Assignment* dare to rest in the discomfort of displacement—of the self, of the heart, of literal location. I don't think I've read a book like this before. Complex and unblinking, with heaps of sorrow and grace, Maldonado has a knack for the impossible, and for making his readers look headlong into it until we all come out the other side more compassionate and honest."—Lynn Melnick

"*The Life Assignment* is, in its own startling terms, an ecology of late capitalist grief. It is also the notebook of a poeta in neoliberal Nueva York, a self-avowed and self-ironizing 'Latinist' in the cold city of wires and data. Ricardo Alberto Maldonado's hemispheric poetics is socially engaged yet rooted in a painful singularity ('I begin *dentro de mí*, / *dentro de nosotros*'). It summons the ghosts of many imbricated (late) modernisms in reflecting on our revanchist moment: Stein's uneasy bodies, Vallejo's wounded yet insurrectionary self-figurations, O'Hara's radically deadpan queer vernacular, Williams's 'poetry of things.' Against the American grain, Maldonado deploys an arsenal of strategic self/mis-translations, unearthing translingual/translocal tensions and correspondences (mamá/mammal, San Juan/New York, love/power). Working through colonial abjection, the poet guides us back to childhood in search of a counternarrative: back to nursery rhymes, to traumatic post-memory, to war and illness, to a mother's love and a father's decay, to the rage and wisdom of same-sex love. Here, the modernist trope of the city in ruins also becomes a post-hurricane elegy for the author's native Puerto Rico, in a desolate feedback loop of individual and collective hunger ('and the city burned with a mighty famine'). Still, amid the 'clattering' of empire, Maldonado finds both punchlines ('Dear Administrator, I will message in a while') and visionary lifelines: the 'water-cradles' and 'slit light' for which we live. This outstanding first book, merciless in its beauty and wit, is a 'schema / for our lapsed world,' a way to make sense of our 'somber city' and 'the grief / we happen to be around.'"—Urayoán Noel

"Ricardo Alberto Maldonado burns language down to the fever, emerges us from the verse, and christens us with high lyric density. 'The capacity for words is debt; its history is arrogance, / a fundamental economy in dark,' writes Maldonado in *The Life Assignment*, a collection whose devastating precision is only matched by its capacity to rebuild tenderness from the ashes." —Raquel Salas Rivera

"'I'd like to think I am trying to keep up, / anyhow, with my rage,' says the speaker of 'Love Poem,' in Ricardo Alberto Maldonado's breathtaking debut, *The Life Assignment*. What is the life assignment? We each have our own and must carry it with us all our days, tinkering over it and revising it, understanding that it necessarily constricts us just as much it guides us. These poems stir inside the brooding atmospheres, workplaces, conference rooms, studio apartments, kitchens, phone calls, inboxes and other stale cavities of late-capitalism, clearing exquisite swaths of language and image that combine the precision of a still-life with the gestural elegance of an open air ceremony. In Maldonado's poems we catch glimpses of Stein, Borges, Shakespeare, Dante ('Midway in the life of our journey we turned / to the console for a slide show') and Woolf, but just as we return our attention to literary history in these moments of intertextuality, we are continually reminded to keep an eye on our precarious present: 'my country, you whimpered under fog. I awoke to the tender / sound of seashells on the radio.' This bilingual collection asks us to consider how we as readers and citizens reconcile self and state, body and landscape, desire and capital, language and communication: 'I pored over / the fuselage, going on in a grey suit / towards roses. I breathless (meanwhile) the air from the head itself, I breathe—.'" —Emily Skillings

THE LIFE ASSIGNMENT

RICARDO ALBERTO MALDONADO

FOUR WAY BOOKS
TRIBECA

Copyright © 2020 Ricardo Alberto Maldonado

No part of this book may be used or reproduced in any manner without written permission except in the case of brief quotations embodied in critical articles and reviews.

"January Morning" By William Carlos Williams, from *THE COLLECTED POEMS: VOLUME I, 1909-1939*, copyright ©1938 by New Directions Publishing Corp. Reprinted by permission of New Directions Publishing Corp.

Library of Congress Cataloging-in-Publication Data

Names: Maldonado, Ricardo Alberto, author. | Maldonado, Ricardo Alberto. Poems. Selections. | Maldonado, Ricardo Alberto. Poems. Selections. Spanish.
Title: The life assignment / Ricardo Alberto Maldonado.
Description: Tribeca : Four Way Books, [2020] | Some poems followed by Spanish translations.
Identifiers: LCCN 2019054594 | ISBN 9781945588549 (trade paperback)
Subjects: LCGFT: Poetry.
Classification: LCC PS3613.A435223 L54 2020 | DDC 811/.6--dc23
LC record available at https://lccn.loc.gov/2019054594

This book is manufactured in the United States of America and printed on acid-free paper.

Four Way Books is a not-for-profit literary press. We are grateful for the assistance we receive from individual donors, public arts agencies, and private foundations.

This publication is made possible with public funds from the National Endowment for the Arts

and from the New York State Council on the Arts, a state agency,

We are a proud member of the Community of Literary Magazines and Presses.

CONTENTS

I Give You My Heart Os doy mi corazón   3
Layaway   5
Poorly Given Miserias   6
Exit, with the Body   11
In Defense of the Life Assignment En defensa de la vida asignada   12
A Few Things Are Explained to Me Me explican algunas cosas   14
Self-Criticism as an Act of Love Autogestión como acto de amor   17
Mi mamá me ama   20
Envoi   24
Love Poem   25
Legislation with Regard to Life 26
Heterosexuality as Custom   27
Leftovers   28
The Rent   29
I, Ricardo, Detached from the Human Ricardo Yo, Ricardo, separándome del humano Ricardo   30
For Love   32
Dinner Special   33
One Fish, Two Fish, Three Fish Un, dos, tres pescados   35
Someone Else's Television   39
The City   40
His Life in Foreclosure   41
TI-83   42
Habemus Lux   43
Set Up Request   46
A Mistranslation of My Name Sobre la traducción de mi nombre   47
A Bird for Felipe, a Bird for Damián Un pájaro para Felipe, un pájaro para Damián   49
The Commodities Market El mercado de materia prima   51
Morning is Morning   55
Project for the Hands   56
Modern Guilt   57
When We Were Mortal   58

Logarithms for Tinderbox   59

Aquatics Period   60

Youth Novels   61

Early Rhetoric and Composition   62

Lesionado   63

Regarding the Life Assignment En cuanto a la vida asignada   65

Voyage to Russia   69

Confessional   70

Bounty   71

Natural History   72

The Symbolism Practice Test   73

Where We Are. Sometimes   74

Last Advertisement for the Life Assignment Último anuncio de la vida asignada   75

Status for the Rest of the Month   77

A Poem for Raquel Un poema para Raquel   78

Entry Level   81

The End of the Economy   82

God or Freud   83

America! America! Las dos Américas   84

Vita Nuova   85

Notes

For what good is it to me
if you can't understand it?
            But you got to try hard—

—William Carlos Williams

My conscience is clear, but that does not make me innocent.

—1 Corinthians 4:4

I GIVE YOU MY HEART OS DOY MI CORAZÓN

I find myself on my feet with fifteen leaves.
Everything carries its own light on the walls.

I woke up to slaughter, my heart opening
to cemeteries of moon—

the parasites, the drizzle. The mud crowning
the undergrowth with immense sadness.

I knew death when I dressed
in my uniform.

I found the index of solitude: my country
in its legal jargon, its piety, its fiction—

Yes. It loves me, really.

I give my blood as the blood of all fish.

Me encuentro de pie con quince hojas.
Brilla todo en los muros.

Desperté en su sacrificio: mi corazón se abría
entre cementerios de luna—

los parásitos, la llovizna. El lodo coronando
la maleza con mustios grandes.

Supe de mi muerte al vestir
de uniforme.

Encontré el índice de soledad: mi país
en su jerga legal, su piedad, su ficción—

Sí. Me quiere, de verdad.

Doy mi sangre como la sangre de todos los peces.

LAYAWAY

First, we would give in to disloyalty
with slack exchanges.

We were figuring what it might be like to live
knowing, intimately, conflicts with size.

Look, my life is not what I would like it to be.
This year, mornings imply an act of bravery.

Look, the window displays are changing.
We could prove what we have yet to dispraise.

All the males have mated and move on
in the city's red gloss.

POORLY GIVEN MISERIAS

We drink milk with minor courage
born of poverty—
                    we'd learned much from books: every day would carry
epistemological
                        imperatives
                                with moccasins to our feet.
        Survival would depend on fidelity to internal
revenue, on observance
                    of parsimony. We would try
to make our way—

orange rinds decayed at the table;
                            the bread began to grow stale.

        We awaken to visions, risk surrender
to exact change.

We consume yet live in abundance,
                            dream of metamorphoses
and self-government
                before the white of eggs.

Lying in bed, we would parse circular deals
                        for indicators of the market's villainy.
Timidly we paced

over foundations and used interpretation

for the octopus tin.

In winter, socks were thicker.

Water at arm's length—we washed underarms,
washed feet with the fury

of lapsed prudery. A right hand probed
the left with uncoordinated

feel for its surface.

In the bath, we would pilfer the toothpaste.

We began to be simple again

yet ceased to be surprised by anything

we would produce.

We yielded to the tide
of urine in the morning, suppressed
lymph—the concentrate
would trickle down to residue.

On the mat, we would bend
to new posture

in the effort of thinking, to have more

to tell of, surely, more

of love, more to understand,
to present something
hopeful, instead, something emblematic
of improved life.

Bebíamos leche con coraje escaso
nacido de nuestra pobreza—
aprendimos de los libros: cada día sugería
su obligación
epistemológica
con mocasines en nuestros pies.
Nuestra supervivencia dependía de fidelidad al ingreso
interno, en la práctica
de mezquindad. Vamos haciendo de
nuestro propio camino—

una cáscara de naranja pudriéndose en la mesa;
el pan se ha endurecido.

Despertamos por visiones, arriesgamos nuestra rendición
al cambio exacto.

Consumimos, pero vivimos en abundancia,
soñando con metamorfosis
y autocontrol

ante claras de huevo.

Acostados en la cama, buscamos en los especiales del día
                    un indicador de villanía en el mercado.

Tímidamente, medimos nuestros pasos
                    sobre fundaciones e interpretamos
                        la latita de pulpo.

En invierno, nuestros calcetines son gruesos.
                    Agua sobre el brazo, agua en nuestras axilas, agua
sobre nuestros pies en su furia
                    de piedad recaída. Una mano derecha sondeando
la izquierda, sintiendo su superficie
                        de manera descoordinada.
En el baño, despreciamos la crema de dientes.

Empezamos a vivir simplemente otra vez
                    sin sorprendernos por nada
                        que habríamos producido.

Rendidos a la corriente
        de orina en la mañana: linfa
suprimida—el concentrado
        escurre su último residuo.

Nos doblamos sobre el colchón, con postura mejorada
en el esfuerzo de pensar, de tener más.

Podremos contar, seguramente, más
        de nuestro amor, más para entender,
para presentar algo
        esperanzador, algo emblemático, en cambio,
                                de una vida mejorada.

EXIT, WITH THE BODY

And out of remorse, I would pay
my debt with medicine—

I'm a Latinist, empirically, with my butane
flame. I would

      1. Keep out of all cities
      2. Raid the costume shop marvelously for Clarence's head
      3. Speak seditiously in society

—yet I would pull verdicts and revelation from *Life*.
                              And on the Internet

I browse for an answer to the coarseness
of the age, the erotics of the West I now give as émigré.

When in doubt, I go to the dictionary.
I put the utensils in the sink.

      The fish dressed in newspaper burn in my reply—
two quietly listening minds hush, feeling, constantly, nostalgia
for the world.

IN DEFENSE OF THE LIFE ASSIGNMENT
EN DEFENSA DE LA VIDA ASIGNADA

I started at the surface, feeling about my face,
the low jawbone my mother had given me
as weapon against austerity. Two decades before,
my father had died. I was desperate under summer's
isosceles. A fragile machine descended
with a yellowing haze on the city.
Whom had I been then, but the sediment inside
that thing I named Ricardo Alberto?
Blessed is he, blessed in the reddening
of medical pins, blessed under fluorine yolks.
I venerated my mother at Centro Médico, her prayer cards
at midnight, the saffron of her blood tearing as it coursed,
a thick mass on concrete inside coral.
Mother, today it snows in another city besieged by comet tails.
You breathed that day, the sharp instrument of men
on your heart—waded, they waded, I remember the wings
of your lungs. It was midnight when I went in search of angels
in the shoes of the sick near the gates of heaven.
On the seventh day, we all take repose in the Kingdom
of the Sick. Blessed are they, blessed the cold comfort of a wind
rushing over teeth, blessed the long corridors
of heaven, blessed the gelatin in refrigerators,
the instant coffee, blessed our sentence of silver, of flowers.
Blessed may they be, blessed.

Empecé al ras, tanteando en mi rostro
el mentón bajo que me había entregado mi madre
como rango contra la austeridad. Dos décadas atrás,
había muerto mi padre. Yo lloraba bajo el isósceles
de junio. Una maquina frágil como niebla amarilla
de estrellas había descendido sobre la ciudad.
¿Quién habré sido aquella vez, además del sedimento dentro
de algo que había llamado Ricardo Alberto?
Bienaventurado sea, bienaventurado en el rojo
fijo y aséptico de alfileres, bienaventurado bajo las yemas de flúor.
Veneré a mi madre en Centro Médico, sus estampitas a media
noche, el azafrán de sangre que rasgaba su curso de masa espesa
sobre el concreto de coral.
Madre, hoy nieva en otra ciudad bajo colas de cometas.
Apenas respirabas aquel día con los instrumentos ásperos
de hombres en tu corazón. Bogando, bogando, recuerdo las alas
de tu pulmón. Eran las doce cuando salí en búsqueda de ángeles
entre los zapatos de los enfermos cerca de las puertas del cielo.
Era el séptimo día cuando se tomaba la siesta en el Reino
de los Enfermos. Bienaventurados sean, bienaventurado el rumor
frío acogedor sobre los dientes, bienaventurados los largos pasillos
de los cielos, bienaventurada la gelatina en los refrigeradores,
el café instantáneo. Bienaventurados en su condena de plata y flor.
Bienaventurados sean.

A FEW THINGS ARE EXPLAINED TO ME
ME EXPLICAN ALGUNAS COSAS

It was five o'clock when paper handkerchiefs descended
over the ocean's surge—
                    one ocean varnished by oil in the morning, fish
under the surge's blades.

My country, you whimpered under fog. I awoke to the tender
sound of seashells on the radio.

I knelt by myself and listened: your flat skeleton, large skeleton,
would group at the back.

Come, you murmured over canned goods. *Come. I will tell you
everything—*

clay seeps onto roots, roots drawn by salt, roots crowned
by trees. The cords unravel from the flesh of trees, unravel
by storm shutters. *Come.*

See the roads brim with red poppy, roads tracked
by green serpents
                    ((a la víbora, víbora / de la mar, de la mar))
I tendered nine eggs before the ignorant lion
of exile, who nodded.

At five in the morning, everything seemed to be made of lime—

one torso shrouded by magnolia, one torso under vulgar peal
of grey morgues, and the fish.

A las cinco de la mañana, descendían sobre olas pañuelos
de papel
         —ese océano revestido por aceite en la mañana, los peces
bajo el filo de olas.

Pueblo mío, gemías bajo niebla cuando desperté
con el ruido tierno de caracolas en radios.

Me arrodillé para escucharte—tu esqueleto gordo
pero raso se agrupaba a tus espaldas.

Venid, dijiste sobre enlatados. *Venid. Os contaré algo*—

el lodo sangraba sus raíces en sal, se coronaban de árboles, desenredaban
cuerdas encarnadas de los árboles
bajo tormenteras. *Venid.*

Ver las calles colmadas de amapolas cortadas, calles rodeadas
de víboras
                ((a la víbora, víbora / de la mar, de la mar)).

Solté mis nueve huevecillos frente al león ignorante
del exilio. Él cabeceaba.

A las cinco de la mañana, me parecía todo estar hecho de cal—

un torso revestido por sudarios de magnolia, un torso desdoblado
bajo vulgar campanadas
de una morgue gris, y los peces.

SELF-CRITICISM AS AN ACT OF LOVE
AUTOGESTIÓN COMO ACTO DE AMOR

The loveseat, my familiar, had me half-numb.

I made the sign at the rim of the clearing

                                        outside on the fire escape,

where I would toss Marlboros out
in the dream of discipline. Milk in a bottle heating

                                in the sun.
I prayed, likely infected
by the warm climate

in the walk-up and the home inside it

where I read a book I would. And the pines keeping roots
nocturnal.

I would rise with my spectacles, light-headed and presexual.

My pallid face made me think of the fabric
on my chest,

pronouncing my fear
beyond words, mad to be in my flesh for one last
minute—

one thing I made by being there, waiting to find my home
by the curve

in the highway and the bridge,

day and night in Manhattan, the borough in the wind.

Sobre el sofá, con mi espíritu, me encontraba medio adormecido.

Crucé mis dedos al persignarme cerca del borde claro
                                    de la escalera de incendios

para desechar los Marlboros
en un sueño de disciplina. La leche en su botella calentaba
                                    bajo sol.

Oré, probablemente afectado
por el clima cálido

en el apartamento sin ascensor en su interior

donde leía lo que podría haber leído. Los pinos guardando de sus raíces
en un nocturno.

    Me habría levantado con mis anteojos, ligero en mente y presexual.

Mi cara pálida pensando sobre la tela
de mi pecho,

pronunciaba algo sobre mi miedo
más allá de las palabras, enojado con mi propia carne, propia piel, en un último
minuto—

algo adicional figuré estando allí, esperando hacer de mi hogar
por la curva

frente al expreso y su puente,
día y noche en Manhattan, la ciudad en el viento.

MI MAMÁ ME AMA

I have a moon. I had six mothers
in my poverty.

Is this all I have for myself?
I was born, like everyone, in a house
with one door.

I have memories
to revise.

No doubt, you'll find
the expiration date.
Mi mamá me ama. I laid waste to my health
in the walls of her heart, while regretting
this analogy
for the labor of a body.

I had a house with three windows.

I remembered her
alone with her memories of youth,
the deep-hearted course
of one rough word turned
judgment in my blood—mother.

As for her, this is the truth:
when she cries
for her mother, I dismantle all walls
to extract her with one word
—mother.

I learn her sacrifice
and grace.

I had one moon. Mother, teach me
when to seek out.

I'll note the expiration date.

That's how I talked while my mother,
with fruit, fed me.

Tengo una luna. Tuve seis madres
en la pobreza.

¿Esto es todo de mí mismo?
Nací, como todos, en una casa
con una puerta.

Tengo recuerdos
por corregir.

Sin duda, encontrarás fecha de vencimiento.
Mi mamá me ama. He estropeado mi salud
en las paredes de su corazón, arrepentido
por esta analogía
para el funcionamiento del cuerpo.

Tuve una casa con tres ventanas.

Recordé que se encontraba
sola con sus recuerdos de juventud, el curso
coronario
de su palabra ruda, vuelta juicio
en sangre—madre.

En cuanto a mi madre, esta es mi verdad:
cuando ella llora
por la suya, desmantelo todas las paredes
para extraerla con una palabra
—madre.

Sabré de su sacrificio,
de su gracia.

Tuve una luna. Mamá, enséñame
a entender.

Sin duda, encontraré fecha de vencimiento.

Así hablaba yo mientras mi madre,
con frutas, me alimentaba.

ENVOI

We are lost on the bed,
an arm cut off by an abstraction.

Old pox, you
and your shirt sleeve.

Yet be careful when you walk there
(outside, the live oaks).

How late, Ricardo, how dark
        and late already.

LOVE POEM

Our somber city of meds & the grief
we happen to be around

—and want. What I think is I would not understand
whom he has loved because I would want ours.

Problems were we were adolescent
in homosexual love, the usual history
of loss, profit.

I'd like to think I am trying to keep up,
anyhow, with my rage.

LEGISLATION WITH REGARD TO LIFE

After sleep would tender its coherence

of thought

      were we careful for each other   it would

matter more that hope in having

      because it offered us no wealth

with insolence we learned this—

            going without

I would concentrate on being there   meanwhile

the sky congests with the work of late fires

HETEROSEXUALITY AS CUSTOM

A sense of men's privacy at the meal,
with extravagant uniform—

they recede in a calming way before men
breach, before men resign
the chance to tender their love of human history,

exhausted by desire in the dangerous
ceremony of love,

using an inside voice when the activity begins—
the search accompanied by sleeplessness,

drink, and of course, the addictive life,
with different contingencies for the commute.

Peace, peace, Mercutio, peace—thou talk'st of men's urgency
and absolute diligence—men consumed

by enmity, and what they meant to retrieve,
the milk now set to expire.

LEFTOVERS

Midway in the life of our journey we turned
to the console for a slide show.

There is much to be seen everywhere:

what San Juan would favor three years from now,
divesting of realty in the financial district.

We feel important in no specific way.

A casserole belatedly served in a basement—

then our second waking
by touch, a thought of the body's license.

The capacity for words is debt; its history is arrogance,
a fundamental economy in dark.

THE RENT

The potatoes on the plate would give way
to symbols for the emotion. We would prosper beyond our vision

for the life assignment, and guided by mailings,
we would thumb through invitations

to experience digestion's early victory
over pleasant chlorination.

Otherwise, distance remains unclear. The bridges signal
to our city's execution.

Capitalism is inescapable. There will be time
for general infirmity.

A light for the times is available inside, with currency
for transport.

I, RICARDO, DETACHED FROM THE HUMAN RICARDO
YO, RICARDO, SEPARÁNDOME DEL HUMANO RICARDO

In youth, they left me by onion
roots to draft an inner life
as reserve for the state—
with a deep throbbing I deviated,
I feel from dignity and calm. I,
anxiety grabbed me
with sciatica, although I recited poems
at a stone's throw, inside the machine
elevator. The clattering of the empire / its capital
an arsenal of pain, it made for a rough
odor. *Now can you see the monument?* I pored over
the fuselage, going on in a gray suit
toward roses. I breathless (meanwhile) the air
from the head itself, I breathe—
                    ((Radio Oro. Son las 5:27 en San Juan.))
They gifted me from previous life
an illumination inside the chest.

Cuando joven, me dejaron que entre cebollas
se formara en mí vida interior
como reserva de estado,
con los latidos siento que desvío
de dignidad, de calma. Yo,
la ansiedad me agarró

30

con dolores de ciática, aunque recitaba poemas
como guerras a pedradas dentro de los ascensores
y máquinas. El parloteo del imperio / su capital
un arsenal de dolor, pero de mal olor
hecho. *¿Puedes ver el monumento?* Vertido sobre
el fuselaje, yendo de traje gris a atrapar
rosas. Yo sin aliento (mientras) aire
del propio cráneo respiro—
        ((Radio Oro. Son las 5:27 en San Juan.))
Dejaron en mi vida anterior
una iluminación dentro del pecho.

FOR LOVE

My life in the lavatory for self-examination
and shampooing—already I would sense the coherence of the floor,

a mythos for Vodka, greased bag
of peanuts.

3:30 a.m. stirs in navy slacks and the silver linden, fair
over my head.

Bewildered by the exercise, I would meditate, sick with a palsy. The spirit
moves, founders on myself, so I keep calm.

The earth hardened against me,
but for the president on his dais in the screen, heavy after bread-wine,
bearable as cattle.

DINNER SPECIAL

Unable to begin, under the incandescent
ongoingness of this.

Late capitalism would give bitter
fruit its malignancy.

And I, with the pretense of wholesomeness
in the last of the clean underwear, would need episodes

of sentiment and impure habits.

I, too, find myself with inferred courage, ready for loyalty
as the Republic frays with adventure of ardor.

Maybe I perceived once I would be taken to the Sea
of the Great Multitudes.

I buy bread that we may eat three pennyworths of barley,
two small fish in grass, fish in corn.

When I awoke with a sharp tooth before dawn,
the perennials kept to disarray

on a plate my hunger drove me to.

I filled my belly with the husks. I knew in the flesh
the youth begins to want,

before I departed to the mount myself alone.

ONE FISH, TWO FISH, THREE FISH
UN, DOS, TRES PESCADOS

Who has been wandering
by my side?

His impoverished hand on wheat, I remember of him
in the drying, the humidity:

water from pebbled seas—Woolf's waves.

I begin. You begin. We begin often. How strange is the Kingdom
of Heaven.

Whose noise tracks by its own fire? Fifteen birds, plastered
in lemon, in lemon and the poetry of things? I get to negotiate with souls?

Every movement in that world of origin
supposes one same loss.

Let us take honey, take nougat; not for that
I'm innocent. One fish, two fish, three fish in fern
lakes, greening

in the cold, bodied in mud, wires and all things lost
to salt—

but I won't do, I won't do more
in my leather shoes. Begin again: seas, red seas, red seas, red seas. Rags
of wars, wars, wars.

Have we begun? One. Two. Three by chalk, three
by mineral. But I won't know, nor I won't be absolved.

Start over: a femur crooks over rags—red rags, rags of war, rags of the sea.
Rough tree, take count of your heart. Take seven, blue sevens by chalk—

it is winter. Then it was winter, a dampness
in red.

¿Quién es ese que deambuló
de mi lado?

Recuerdo su mano pobre frente al trigo de su sol seco
y su humedad,

la humedad, el agua de mar, un mar pedregoso—las olas
de Woolf.

Empiezo. Empiece. Empecemos. Qué extraño es el Reino
de los Cielos.

¿Será que arde en el ruido? ¿Quince pájaros de yeso
y limón, la poesía de las cosas? ¿Con las almas puedo
negociar?

Cada movimiento en ese mundo de origen
supone su misma pérdida.

Llevemos, pues, turrón y miel; no por eso
quedo absuelto. Uno. Dos. Tres de esos

peces en lago de helechos
verdes,

un frío poblado de barro, de alambres, cosas perdidas
en su sal—

pero no hago, no hago más

de zapatos en charol. Empecemos otra vez: mares, mares rojos, mares
rojos, mares rojos. Trapos de guerras, guerras, guerras.

¿Ya empezamos? Uno. Dos. Un tres en su tiza, tres
en su mineral. Pero no sé, no sé quedar absuelto.

Empecemos encorvados de huesos de las espaldas con trapos, trapos
rojos, trapos de guerra, trapos de mar.

Árbol de semillas, ya empalmado en rojo su pegamento. Contemos
ya el séptimo en tiza azul, pero árbol—

es invierno. Entonces fue inverno, su rojo
sudoroso.

SOMEONE ELSE'S TELEVISION

Many of us overcome eventual flaws
to keep to the ones we love.

We pay the impenetrable cost of evening.

We miss the way we are more so
than our friends, and we don't need

to be saved, not really. Dinners start

with "you have loved"—every why, in itself,
heavenly with wretchedness

reaches us blindly. These, our stories,

we consume in silence. We have use for this
impulse and find ourselves romantic

about customs, yet it helps to be proactive

about guilt and the adjectives assigned
to us in lovemaking (reckless, confused).

THE CITY

—I am almost 37, but I'm 36
inside my very own skin, doing the decent

thing, spreading out over linen with the edibles
of a friendlier house.
2 a.m. laundromat, the air signaling.

Winter cold at my thighs. The alley frays with aerial wires, bathing me
with data.

The city greys, dry on my neck, easy and raw
from my match. I cough out.

I bring myself to the senses, smart once clean,
thrice clean on Wednesdays

—my substance riotous with living

and the city burned with a mighty famine
of that land.

HIS LIFE IN FORECLOSURE

Astray—with cereal from wheat fields inside me I savor one word
for it.

I could be glossy in my youth, sock-footed, polished
in my shoes.

Washington Heights while the country was sleeping—

night after night M bends toward Aurelius, the light softens
the mouse in his hands.

That night I misremembered my book of changes: all the way up,
in the summer, one mammal wavered in from the weather.

TI-83

I came to life in Physics
101 and played to Middle Important
places—

    1-day Callaway and English
AB. As usual, to myself own and to any,

    the dream shies, falsely Catholic and spongy.
My accent would change, marbling
              like gravy on white bread.

Wisdom made interesting sorrow of my inbox.
                That's the stuff, in general, I would
try for—butter
      in paradise,
      golden lemon-yellow, unlike advertising
      commending fruit.

HABEMUS LUX

"I was afraid. I looked out the window and I saw a cat swimming," Ismael
said. — in "The image of our poverty," *Primera Hora*, Puerto Rico:
9/26/17

And then there was light, and the cats bathed because there was light
to bathe under. And washing machines and ice factories, because the
light was noble. And the cats were fecund, filling the waters with little
sausage cans and empty water bottles. And there was power at the
grocery stores, power at the tolls, power at the Costco, power at the
shopping mall, power at the filling stations, power at the outlet stores.
And all the fixtures in children's bedrooms shone bright in a paradise,
because there was light in the darkness. And it was late, and it was
morning for all luminaries, because it was the Eleventh Month.

This is the book for the generations of Cats. These are the generations
that will serve them: they were Abram's Cats; Agar gave birth to her
cats, but the cats were afraid, because they were naked in the darkness.
Cats facing trees; Cats wearied by the cold; Cats in the rubble; Cats
roofing again; one cheese slice for a cat's breakfast.

And one cat said: it's not good that the cats be alone; I will help them,
and she took flesh from her rib and closed the wound in that place
to make something of it. And Cat begat according to her image, and
named her Light—and as Cat named her, that was her name, Light,
because she was noble: *Light in the Morning; Light in the Darkness;*

Bloom, Light, Alum-Bright! And that's what Cat had done in a great way.

The days of Cat after begetting Light were four thousand six hundred and forty-five. And the total number of days that the cats lived was four thousand six hundred and forty-five when flowers bloomed in an orange burst. And it was late for the cats, Cat in the darkness, Cat in the morning—Day One.

"A mí me dio miedo. Yo miré por la ventana y vi un gato nadando", admitió Ismael. —en "La imagen de nuestra pobreza," *Primera Hora*: 9/26/17

Entonces llegó la Luz, y los gatos se bañaban porque hubo luz para bañarse. Y lavadoras y fábricas de hielo, porque la luz era noble. Fueron fecundos, los gatos, llenando las aguas de los mares con latas de salchicha y botellitas NAYA. Y hubo luz en los colmados, luz en los peajes, luz en el Costco, luz en Plaza, luz en la Shell, luz en los Outlets, y esas manzanitas enchufadas en los cuartos de los niños brillaban como Paraíso, porque hubo luz en las tinieblas. Y fue tarde, y fue la mañana en que hubo lumbreras, porque era el undécimo mes.

Este es el libro de las generaciones de gatos. Estas son las generaciones que le servirán: eran los Gatos de Abram; Agar dió a luz a Gatos, pero los gatos tuvieron miedo, porque estaban desnudos en las tinieblas. Gatos frente a árboles; Gatos baldados de frio; Gatos entre los escombros; Gatos tejando de nuevo; una lasca de queso para el desayuno de Gatos.

Y un gato dijo: No es bueno que los Gatos estén solos; les haré una ayuda. Y tomó la carne de una de sus costillitas y cerró la carne en ese lugar para ser algo suyo. Entonces el Gato engendró conforme a su imagen, y le puso por nombre Luz y como el Gato le llamó, ése fue su nombre, Luz, porque era noble: Luz en la Mañana, Luz en las Tinieblas, Lucecita, ¡Alumbra, Lumbre de Alumbre! Y fue así todo lo que los Gatos habían hecho en gran manera.

Los días de Gatos después de haber engendrado Luz fueron cuatro mil seisientos cuarenta y cinco. Y el total de los días que los gatos vivieron fue de cuatro mil seisientos cuarenta y cinco cuando germinaron flores en un estallido naranja. Y fue tarde para los Gatos, fueron Gatos en las tinieblas, fueron Gatos en la mañana, un día.

SET UP REQUEST

It is difficult—

not being hard on myself, but regardless
        of the hyphenated

mind, I quit.

        You'll think the team of linoleum
halos were sick of it, also.

     If you were to ask
me, I mind always the living as we are now,

       uncontrollable and moored
by the forms at the desk.

A MISTRANSLATION OF MY NAME
SOBRE LA TRADUCCIÓN DE MI NOMBRE

Vietnam, yesterday's half-moon—three veins
in his childhood singed by sun.

A country like a scrap of skin on which we wrote ourselves:

his flesh, his spirit—a sparrow in hand, metallic dress
as inkwell under my bed,

and a desert of wet tobacco, rose in his lung. My father,
one among assassins.

I came to understand his blood as a river from which we drank
when we were children among tender roots and moss.

I remembered a fable set to glass leaves, my mother in July.
That my sister sleeps.

That my father, Judas toward God, awakened, his stomach distended,
to relieve himself like an animal.

Vietnam, media luna de ayer—tres venas de su niñez
cegadas por el sol.

Un país como trozo de piel sobre el cual escribimos nosotros mismos:

su carne, su espíritu como golondrina entre manos, un traje metálico
como tintero bajo mi cama,

desierto de tabaco húmedo, rosa en su pulmón. Mi padre, uno
entre asesinos.

Comprendí que su sangre era río del cual bebimos antes de ser niños,
entre raíces tiernas y musgo.

Recordé su fábula de selva entre hojas de vidrio. A mi madre
en julio. Que mi hermana duerme.

Que padre despertó una vez, ese Judas de su Dios, con su vientre distendido
mientras orinaba como animal.

A BIRD FOR FELIPE, A BIRD FOR DAMIÁN
UN PÁJARO PARA FELIPE, UN PÁJARO PARA DAMIÁN

A man dies in this world by a fist
of trees, more than by our love.
When I was young, muscles were carved from the minerals
so we could be forgiven.
And yet, at the greeting of the birds,
I loved the work, loved its respite,
with which I wrote, the silt of our fears.
It rains this September in our world.
I've gained more from its wear.
Who am I to be yours in this compulsory
century, but a father, without possessive?
I loved. I loved. I love presently.
I fly its unavoidable flag,
that trade, a match for us in the cold,
a room in September,
our whitening bones, humid
in our melancholy.
There's nothing more to do but make it
ours. I waited with my lamp
to assemble birds for you,
then release them,
as if I were a child, to understand you,
like the fresh water
that washed over my hands.

Un hombre muere en algún mundo por el puño
de un árbol, más que por nuestro amor.
Cuando yo era pequeño, se labró un músculo
de su mineral para ser perdonado.
Y sin embargo, ante el saludo de los pájaros, amé la labor,
su respiro, que escribía con la mugre de nuestras ansias.
Llueve como septiembre en este mundo.
Tengo más por su desgaste.
¿Quién soy yo para ser suyos en este siglo
compulsorio, sino un padre, pero sin posesivo?
Amé. Amé. Yo amo.
Tengo su bandera insoslayable.
Ese oficio para nosotros como fósforo en el frío
en un cuarto de septiembre
con nuestros huesos blancos, húmedos
por la melancolía.
Queda más nada que hacerlo
nuestro. Esperaba con mi lámpara
para inventar pájaros para ustedes
e impulsarlos
como cuando pequeño, para entenderlos,
como el agua fresca
que me dejó las manos.

THE COMMODITIES MARKET
EL MERCADO DE MATERIA PRIMA

Where one finds poetry, one finds the Lord,
God of Epic, a golden instrument on Our Lord's plums, God the body,

pelt of Our Lord, red cap for a red God, tree of the Heavens.

Remember, José Daniel? The God we engraved on our desks?
Christ of Our Lord, Christ of Our Children.

Lord's denominator in the Lord's arithmetic, a pair of children
scissors.

God at our borders, the salt
of Our Lord, God's ocean of cotton, of sugar.

A nickname for God: The Lord Elephant. Lord mule.
Lord's acres. Hospital Lord. Texas for God Alabama.
God's sea of blue tarps.

Our Lord's November. An August for Our God. Roses of God
for the roses.

Clouds for the Lord. Will the Gods
disappear, their arms full of roses?

The wall of our Lord, Our Lord in God's roses,
Lord's wound flowering red.

One heaven of fog clouding faces for heaven of roses—a heaven
for God, Our Lord and the Darkness

of numbers, Lord's icebox, Lord's cages
for the Children of God, an armful of roses

for roses of God, God's labor, God's Wednesdays
as labor and the labor of God.

Donde se encuentre la poesía, se encuentra su Dios
epopeya, el tenedor oro en las ciruelas de Dios, el Dios en su cuerpo,

sus pieles de Dios, su gorro rojo de Dios rojo, el árbol de los cielos.

¿Recuerdas, José Daniel, cuando grabamos al dios en los pupitres?
El Cristo de Dios, el Cristo de los Niños.

Su aritmética, el denominador de Dios, las tijeras
de los niños.

El Dios en las fronteras, la sal
de su Dios, su mar de algodón, de azúcar.

El Dios en su apodo de Dios Elefante. Dios mula.
Los terrenos de Dios. El Dios de hospitales. Un Texas

para el Dios Alabama.
Su mar de carpas azules.

El Dios su noviembre. Su agosto de Dios. Las rosas de Dios
de sus rosas.

¿Desaparecerán
los Dioses con rosas en sus brazos?

El muro de Dios, el Dios en sus rosas,
Dios su llaga de flamboyán.

El cielo estaba encancaranublado, encancaranublado de rosas
de Dios, Dios en sus turbios

números, la hielera de Dios, las jaulas de Dios
de sus niños, sus rosas de manos

de rosas de Dios, su trabajo, su miércoles
de Dios, su trabajo de Dios.

MORNING IS MORNING

I have some explaining to do—

five o'clock and I would speculate
about artichokes and the unfarmed mackerel.

Anyway, the men would present us with a bed of carrot
and potatoes + one cup of broth.

Our husbandry in sharp mustard
suit, laden with trial pieces for the fondue, I had
such friends—

a long time faring all through the West
with my filth and a bouquet of cutlery
where I had put it: by me.

And yet expansive, the things made by the things
I made. And a supervisor hovering behind me. The heaviness
of being.

I am the Name, Jehovah called from the bush. I had visions

of pigeons. And I replied: *Here I am to be called Ishmael and beget.*

PROJECT FOR THE HANDS

I would say—part scattered, part
inclement. I recalled

nothing of the gift. I am glad for the liquor
of knives.

He would smile: matchbox, crowns
of cauliflower

—his dog-drawl.

I could fold my knuckles into the mouth
of a wolf.

It never gets easy,
not ever.

MODERN GUILT

The street chiaroscuro avails us of a preparatory
for telegraphs—

the colophons disperse.

Night appears with yesterday's broadcast
in a piano's monochrome.

The glass from the greenhouse nicks
us toward violence.

We tread toward sleep as inferior
gift—we are mortal as God's sin.

Night lifts us with vials of naphthalene
and the serpent's narrow ardor.

Doctors trade aubades at late hours
inducing relief with prose.

Safe passage: this world takes the place
of those I love.

The leaves swim in
beyond revivals of the moon.

WHEN WE WERE MORTAL

We would set precincts for the gods to assemble
with beasts—

fevers pressured them to chew tobacco
and redden alleys with a criminal will.

Let us not lose each other
in medicinal age,
sipping balms after winds disperse.

Therefore, at the Hospital
for Melancholy,
the lights and telephones hold—

what else for night?

We would express how meek our rites
seem in spite of calendars:

trepans perforate soil, then we repent.

Snow would descend, often by fleets, often as schema
for our lapsed world.

LOGARITHMS FOR TINDERBOX

Much of wood, much of river—
I wish I were a bird to set myself upon the work
of hymning:

hapless about hills out of furnaces out
of the sea for coal.

I am to remember my living ended
as I would be,

hiding my crest somewhere along
ice

and learn from wind reports now obsolete
on the North side.

The radio program patterns umlauts as rain.

AQUATICS PERIOD

Drag us to the water-cradles,
all excerpts of ourselves

bend ungenerous
with the shame we would elicit—

little by little, the trees would
render neutral segments
of rye,

weaned off salt, weaned off whiskey.

The white room in my mind
is rectangular, of thick Technicolor.

Sick of night-caravels,
we would measure our records with iron
from our age.

Freight cars rag the asphalt.

The last trace of monochrome appears
before us.

Bats regroup to blacken alleys
under hood of nightfall.

YOUTH NOVELS

We would cower when pressed
by penance, doctored

with the acetylene of cinemas:
after errands,

with the wherefore
of insides—for whose love,

sir, for whom can we cleanse
ourselves

with a kind of symmetry,
fresh lung?

And the mind
would seize the wild

and perpendicular
earth, appalled

by serial autumns,
at the highways, and in time.

EARLY RHETORIC AND COMPOSITION

The day ancient and invincible—
      my hymns were scrapwood and feeble, camouflage-safe.

Then came benediction,
      rains dissolving screeds in white timber.

It was a sin—remedy from the chance system. Even I would keep

Father from facing my sounds and my care—
                even in his dying.

LESIONADO

Maybe this will be a poem about power—

Reading rereading whatever shape the intelligence
takes:

Somewhere somehow the men the state
Somewhere seems to destroy

Only we should be beautiful and practical
Finding beauty will stand everywhere

Among two Victorias my brothers and I among them
Home for its noun
Home for its soil one two three four I among them

Maybe this is a poem about power
Maybe this is a poem about love.

Tal vez este sea un poema sobre el poder—

Leyendo releyendo cualquier forma que la inteligencia
Pudiese tomar:

De algún modo dónde van hombres el estado
De algún modo les parecer destruir

Sólo debemos ser hermosos y prácticos
Encontrando que durará la belleza en todas partes

Entre dos Victorias mis hermanos y yo
Ese hogar como su sustantivo
Ese hogar en su barro uno dos tres cuatro yo entre ellos

Tal vez este sea un poema sobre el poder
Tal vez este sea un poema sobre el amor.

REGARDING THE LIFE ASSIGNMENT
EN CUANTO A LA VIDA ASIGNADA

As a mammal I prized, prized above all things, shavings
in snow I would pencil under glare
of green shadows.

The homeland is beautiful! ¡La patria es hermosa!

The children moved on, every day, moved on
toward the violence of signs, with their molars.
The children swayed by thrones of chilled honey.

We found seven, Mamá, seven drawers
full of swallows, seven ribbons the children would set lose with pencils,
seven milk teeth, when the rooster cackled.

Would you tell them, Mamá, we found drawers,
drawers for marine times?

Mamá would wake me
before I went to school. We went to school and the ice cream parlor
in the river near the forest
with our swallows, Mamá.

When Mamá cast off her white
doves, it rained and it rained over galleons
made of coral,
traced in lemon iodine, white cloths
swaying in marine struggle.

How beautiful is the homeland! ¡Qué hermosa es la patria!

Seven swaying on cardboard and the homeland,
an insectary in the heart
over the lemon of rivers.

Seven coloring mud, they would color with sand,
wounding themselves with melancholy, Mamá,
driving a littering of leaves
into the water of rivers. *¡De qué color! Which color! Lemon green!*

Seven ankles, seven in casts, seven in plaster,
as they swayed by the river
with three oranges under the glare of the Republic—raise the Republic!

Chilled honey they coughed out when it rained,
Mamá, penciling a river's blue glare, thick molars
for moon,
to peck at that scorpion with joy,
when the rooster cackled.

A la limón, the children moved on, to the lemon, Mamá.
Swaying over moon
of marine monuments—
over the blade of a knife.

Como mamífero amaba, pues, los copos
de nieve figurados bajo el fulgor de tiniebla verde.

¡La patria es hermosa!

Cada día, iban los niños hacia la violencia
de signos, con sus molares. Iban los niños, a mecerse en su trono
de miel helada.

Fueron siete, siete cajones de golondrinas, siete cintas
sin nudos de niños que figuramos,
siete dientes de leche, cuando cacareaba el gallo.

Dígale, Mamá, que encontramos cajones,
cajones para tiempos marinos.

Mamá me levantaba
para ir al colegio. Íbamos al colegio y a la heladería
del río en el bosque
con sus golondrinas, Mamá.

Cuando Mamá levantaba sus blancas
palomas, llovía.
Llovía, Mamá, sobre el galeón de coral
figurado por iodo limón, blancos paños
en su lucha marina.

¡Qué hermosa es la patria!

Fueron siete en mecerse en la patria,
el insectario
del corazón como el limón del río.

Teñían de arena su lodo para herirse, Mamá,
de melancolía, impulsando una hojarasca
en el agua del río. ¡De qué color, verde limón!

Siete tobillos. Fueron siete en yeso
para mecerse por el río con tres naranjas
bajo el fulgor de la República—¡volverla a levantar!

La miel helada tosieron cuando llovía,
Mamá, figurando el río de sus tinieblas azules

con muelas de luna espesa,
para besar ese escorpión de su alegría,
cuando cacareaba el gallo.

A la limón, a la limón iban los niños, Mamá.
A mecerse sobre la luna
sobre monumentos marinos—
a mecerse, como a punta de navaja.

VOYAGE TO RUSSIA

An empirical dream of a sea

of lead, gray and aphonic as a little
                              iron wrist splits

        Revolutionary Man! Man
of Epochs!
                —maybe the fish
        of the soul

redeem us from our workdays.

One o'clock is in need of a reason
        to leave you with the hurt of ages.

Night's kinder to the sorrow
                        of the city.

CONFESSIONAL

It is clear I have no idea of what you'd like me
to do with the results.

I don't know why we should have to talk

because, anyway, other people can't say
                              you can love anymore.

I would remind you of my eventual disobedience—the fire's ways
sans withal,

that minor homicide in boredom's
romance.

As usual, you came as well, a weeks-to-night neutral, rapturous
and immune. Wants to talk about closure.

In any case, thank you for your attention
to this matter.

BOUNTY

> "pero estamos vivos"
> 21 de septiembre de 2017

One: home

Two: home   *dos tres dos tres*   two: Mother.

One *lápiz*. One pen. One ocean between us. Six: Home.

Seven: FEMA: *four thousand more,*
     I recite.

I state I am large; we are to be

larger.   *Uno dos tres siete dieciséis cuatro mil*

más I begin. I begin *dentro de mí, dentro*
de nosotros.

I accuse one man. Two men. Three men. Men men. State
men. I accuse whomever I find I have found.

Mother, I founder.

I want truth: one ocean more, one home more
than a wave is glass.

I am one man larger and savage.
Two men. Three Men. State *four*, mother. State *five*. State

state. Dios nos salve, madre, dios nos salve, dios nos salve.

NATURAL HISTORY

Mild September, though sometimes I washed in water, washed
& prepared fields for my billet.

I felt God walk deep within and forged a tough grief to hurt him.
Wheat turns to coal.

With him night falls in our orphanhood—day and night by uneven fire.

                        Levitation! Mother, would you know
                        the sorrow.

César Vallejo died. Descartes died, and the universe
and I were born to 1981, the voice of adults in the kitchen.

THE SYMBOLISM PRACTICE TEST

I don't mean to be crass, Little
Bird, except I had a thought—I had made it:

windowsills disintegrate into pollen.

I sauntered in by myself for a salad from the mini-fridge.
My parka would deflate
after naming.

Dear Administrator, I will message in a while.

I had a vision. I would prefer how the folks lived up there, honoring the
branch—ruddier
in the wind like the fog

on the elms at the end of the street.

WHERE WE ARE, SOMETIMES

—At bloodletting. Our fathers are caught
On brambles and we owe them

Ourselves, our roots, our patrician
Feature. We are fetched for lessons in cardboard

And spores.

As usual, dogs follow.
Lately our hands are cast from metal.
Only the lamps, upon dissection, answer.

This youth we arch toward—every
Midnight the silver blades shift.

Our fathers, the books
Of cosmonauts—

Mornings in a case and a kind
Of tweed, we fast at a diner of slit light.

LAST ADVERTISEMENT FOR THE LIFE ASSIGNMENT
ÚLTIMO ANUNCIO DE LA VIDA ASIGNADA

Here, in December, snow tends an oxidized tint over my shoes, porous under a caravan of leaves. Sebastián, at seven, the light dims over oatmeal on chicken pox. At thirty, I swallowed one acid thing, which went down my stomach, supplying it with actual weight. I felt herds of calcium in my liver whimpering for herbs in the bedrooms of my fever. You arrived like my two other astronauts dressed in anemones and dark blue wires. Your fingers, a mouthful in the mud of your gums. Giraffes sleep in your room. Rain falls on the wardrobes of all judges. Sea lamps are put out—seven orange caravels under three cardinal points: three for your North, three for your South. Six airplanes under a downpour: ((de olas, in waves, de olas / waves of the sea, / ¡Qué bonitas! How beautiful the waves to navigate)) your bed sheets. Dawn breaks loose of its sand in the taverns of sleep and work.

Acá la nieve de diciembre tenderá su hojalata verde sobre mis zapatos, para hacerse porosa sobre caravanas de hojas. Sebastián, a las siete, se ensombrece el sedimento de avena sobre la varicela. A mis treinta, tragué algo ácido que bajó hasta el estómago, supliéndole peso real. Sentía yo rebaños de calcio en el hígado gimiendo por hierbas en los dormitorios de la fiebre. Llegaste como mis otros dos astronautas en sus anémonas y alambres de azul vino. Tus dedos su bocanada en el lodo de las encías. En tu habitación duermen las jirafas. Cae la lluvia sobre los roperos de los jueces. Se apagaban lámparas del mar—siete carabelas naranjas bajo tres puntos cardinales: tres por tu norte, tres por tu sur. Seis aeroplanos bajo tela de aguacero. ((De olas, las olas, las olas / olas de la mar, / ¡Qué bonitas las olas para navegar!)) tus sábanas. Apenas el alba desprende su desierto de arena sobre tabernas del sueño y del trabajo.

STATUS FOR THE REST OF THE MONTH

9:17 a.m. and the water seems turgidly prohibitive,
would scald me with indifference to the pledges
of toothpaste.

The replacement sofa cedes to my weight
and when I touch my gut in the shower, thoughts are revealed

with little comedic effect: Hurry evening—cigarette
paper, gold in our hands.

Tomorrow, jeans will slip on in 50-degree
weather and my repugnant heart will make me conspicuous
on the train, and later, at the bus station.

A POEM FOR RAQUEL UN POEMA PARA RAQUEL

A poem as bird, a bird of colors, *de colores*
son los pajaritos, we would cast from inside.

Which would bring me to the metaphysical argument—

The body is not a metaphor.
The body is not a metaphor.
The body is not a metaphor.
The body is not a metaphor.

I spot, I spot. Suddenly in night I happen to signal to my body,
my body in silt.

And I would answer, *Here I am*, because metaphors consumed me
and the body

> (his body, her body, their body),

they all burned but were not consumed, but thickened
in tar, praying in the heat—
holy heat, Patron Heat, Creator of the Fruit.
Have I found the poem?

I spot, I spot birds on brambles: one flies, one flies
from us, we cast from us.

> I spot, I spot, I don't know how.

I am Father of God, God of Father, because I was afraid to look, because the body is not a metaphor,

but a body, thought over, healed flesh for its own life.
I had an inviolate ocean—tombstones of flowers.
                              Well, you need all these things.
Here I am, the nitrate
of my armpits. Eat; this is my body
                     which I parted for you;
do it in memory of the body.

Un poema es un pájaro de colores, *de colores son*
los pajaritos que vienen de adentro.
                     Cosa que en mí narra su asunto metafísico—

El cuerpo no es una metáfora.
El cuerpo no es una metáfora.
El cuerpo no es una metáfora.
El cuerpo no es una metáfora.

Veo, veo—sucede a lo largo de la noche en cuerpo sucio, lleno
de metáforas.

Y yo respondo, *Heme aquí,* porque me consumen
las metáforas y su cuerpo
                     (y el de él, y el de ella, y el de ellx)

todxs ardían, pero no se consumían sobre brea
espesa, desaseándo su calor santo, santo patrón, creador del fruto.
¿He encontrado el poema?

Ya veo. Veo sobre zarzas los pájaros: vuela aquél, vuela aquél
de nosotoros.

                      Veo, pero yo no sé.

Yo soy padre de dios, dios del padre, porque tengo miedo de mirar,
                      porque el cuerpo no es una metáfora,

pensé sobre el cuerpo nuestro, curado de su carne viva por lo que es suyo.

Tuve un mar púrpura—camposanto de moriviví.
            Bien, tenéis necesidad de todas estas cosas.
Heme aquí, el nitrato
de las axilas. Comed; esto es mi cuerpo
               que por vosotros es partido;
hacedlo en memoria del cuerpo.

ENTRY LEVEL

Last week's probables left me at a loss
for someone else's élan.

It seems days are stripped of kindness—

absent of clerks and signs of utility, they court
their obsolescence by night.

Herewith the job description:

Enough now. Let go.
Enter Oldsmobiles in the rain.

THE END OF THE ECONOMY

deploys its capital
like an erector set
the invisible hand pierces
numerously from us
onto the paneled wall
a plush wilderness delights
under the pubis
like besieged machinery
hard-trying
in postmodern
orange steel
rising uncommonly discreet
doctoring wealth
for what has ended
but the profound
marbling of a concussion
would earn a formal
splendor
for whose debt we would
prefer like that peculiar mist
that triggers a depression,
but a deformity of it

GOD OR FREUD

Under a sheet of standard count, the wall would make
the actual weight degrade to my touch.

This is the age of industry.

In the avenue of the Republic the populace divests
with facility,

underground, at the locker room, yielding to the shoulder,
to pulse—

a body found within, male and imperially breaking—
sickened and weaned off remorse.

The skin appears under influence—once driven to be pleased,
is now cast with resultant
                on the back, on the mouth on the ground.

AMERICA! AMERICA! LAS DOS AMÉRICAS

In interiors by night-light and by our own
admission, we levitate—

> it is our birthright. Suppose the cargo was brought
> for our welfare: a kind

of instruction toward ill, produce
> we could not afford.

Thoughts about the climate and the waste
> of our prose

disclose the economy of our youth—

there were trees the storm had reserved,
fathers unmannered at the effort.

Our theater confused the gods.

We observed the trees—we never knew the fluttering
> made them distinct.

En su interior, bajo luz nocturna y por admisión
suya, levitan—

> es su derecho. Supongamos su carga es dispensada
> para el bien común:

esa especie de instrucción enferma, como producto
     no sufragado.

Como reflexión de clima, el residuo de su prosa

revela la economía de su juventud—

habían árboles que la tormenta reservó,
adultos maleducados por su esfuerzo.

Su teatro confundió a los dioses.

Observaron los árboles—nunca supieron si su revoloteo
los hizo diferentes.

VITA NUOVA

In the book of the life I have made, my memory would
appear cursed, about halfway, by affairs

and irrational fears: Capitalism is inescapable. We were popular
with men we knew.

Light strikes my white tennis shorts,
and life feels life in a city for each still visible and waiting.

This is the 21st century.

We never leave when life is elsewhere. The clemency of men disappears
as does the light, tarring the roofs.

NOTES

Translations and intentional mistranslations are mine. Poems presented in both languages were written in Spanish then rendered into English. Whereas the process of translating work dictated some changes in the original, at no time were concessions made to the language of (our current) Empire.

"I Give You My Heart Os doy mi corazón" was written the week of September 20, 2017, after hurricane María made landfall in Puerto Rico.

Several poems, including "Exit, with the Body," use language from William Shakespeare's plays, others from The King James Bible. Language in "A Few Things Are Explained to Me" is taken from Pablo Neruda's "I Explain a Few Things," as well as lines from "La víbora de la mar," a popular children's game in Puerto Rico and Latin America. "Mi mamá me ama" retains language from a failed response (mine) to Mahmoud Darwish's indispensable poem, "I Belong There." "In Defense of the Life Assignment En defensa de la vida asignada" follows a similar strategy. The translators of Darwish's poem are Munir Akash and Carolyn Forché, with Sinan Antoon and Amira El-Zein.

Most of the poems in this book, including "Leftovers," were written during Puerto Rico's decades-long economic crisis. For educational resources and more information on the sources of the crisis, readers are encouraged to access the Puerto Rico Syllabus: www.puertoricosyllabus. com.

"I, Ricardo, Detached from the Human Ricardo Yo, Ricardo, separándome del humano Ricardo" takes its title from a line in Henri Cole's "At the Grave of Elizabeth Bishop" and includes a line from Elizabeth Bishop's poem, "The Monument."

"Habemus Lux" references a newspaper article published six days after Hurricane María made landfall in Puerto Rico.

"Morning is Morning" takes its title from Bruce Springsteen's "You're Missing."

"Regarding the Life Assignment En cuanto a la vida asignada" references "A la limón," a popular children's song in Puerto Rico.

"Bounty" begins with a text message a friend sent out the morning of September 20, 2017; it was received a day later. The poem's title references Donald J. Trump's presidential visit to Puerto Rico on October 3, 2017.

Language in "Natural History" is taken from Yvette Siegert's translations of César Vallejo's work, as well as Ngo Tu Lap's *Black Stars,* as translated by Martha Collins and the author.

"Where We Are. Sometimes" owes its title to John Ashbery's "Our Youth."

"A Poem for Raquel Un poema para Raquel" references a line from Frank O'Hara's "At Joan's."

ACKNOWLEDGMENTS

Dedico este libro a la memoria de mi padre, José Raúl Maldonado; y a mi madre, Victoria; a Diana, José, Roberto, Victoria y Viviana; y a mis sobrinos: Damián, Felipe y Sebastián. Amo.

I also dedicate this book to the memory of Lucie Brock-Broido, Deborah Digges, and Father Francis P. Golden, S.J., my first poetry teachers.

For opening the doors at Tufts, I remain indebted to Lee Edelman, Christina Sharpe, Jonathan Wilson, and Adriana Zavala. At Columbia: Timothy Donnelly, Tracy K. Smith, Marjorie Welish, and Monica Youn. At the Poetry Project and Q|A|M: Stacy Szymaszek. And the visiting faculty at 92Y, especially Catherine Barnett, Cynthia Cruz, Emily Fragos, francine j. harris, Matthea Harvey, Alberto Manguel, Idra Novey, Kathleen Ossip, Molly Peacock, Helen Vendler, and Ann Washburn. At CantoMundo: Ada Limón and Daniel Borzutzky. And to Lynn Melnick—mil gracias, Lynn.

For encouragement and guidance during the writing of this book: Matthew Pennock, Yvette Siegert, and Erica Wright. My gratitude to Hafizah Geter and Camille Rankine. To Libby Burton, Wil Lobko, and Maud Poole. Also to Stephanie Anderson, Marie Elia, Julia Guez, Marwa Helal (!), Erica Mena, Billy Merrell, Danniel Schoonebeek, Emily Skillings, Christina Quintana, Annabelle Yeeseul Yoo, Samantha Zighelboim, and my classmates at Columbia. Also thanks to Will Brewer, Kelly Forsythe, David Burr Gerrard, MC Hyland, Sam Ross, sam sax, and Ryann Wahl.

For the gift of corroboration, my deep appreciation to Raquel Salas Rivera (♥), Denice Frohman, Urayoán Noel, and Carina del Valle Schorske. To Beca Alderete Baca, Celeste Mendoza, Deborah Paredez and the CantoMundo family: administrators, faculty and fellows— bendiciones. Mi agradecimiento a Diana Marie Delgado, Sheila Maldonado, Yesenia Montilla, Christina Olivares, and Peggy Robles-Alvarado.

To my colleagues at the Unterberg Poetry Center, especially Bernard Schwartz and Wendy Salinger; to Sophie Herron and Ava Lehrer. At Four Way Books: Bridget Bell, Clarissa Long, Ryan Murphy, and Martha Rhodes. I am also grateful for the support of 92Y, the New York Foundation for the Arts, Queer|Arts|Mentorship and the T.S. Eliot Foundation.

Gracias a Jaime Alberty, José Daniel Aponte, Maria Celeste Colberg, Juan Horta, Yamile Martí, Gabrielle Olivencia, a Alfredo y Andrés Richner. A Mariana Ramos Ortiz, por hacer de mi sueño tu portada y por todo tu trabajo.

My thanks to the editors of the following journal, magazines and anthologies in which these poems, sometimes in earlier versions, first appeared: *Academy of American Poets' Poem-a-Day, Anomalous, Argos Books, Article, Associative Press, Boston Review, The Common, Denver Quarterly, DIAGRAM, The Equalizer, Explosion-Proof!, Guernica, InDigest, jdbrecords, Kweli Journal, Los Angeles Review of Books, Love Among the Ruins, The Offing, Oversound, Perihelion, PEN Poetry Series, Philadelphia Review of Books, Pinwheel, Please Excuse This Poem: 100 New Poets for the Next Generation, Poems for a Political Disaster, Poetry Magazine, The Poetry Project, Poetry Society of America, Public Pool, The Rumpus, Sidebrow, Slice, Spinning Jenny, Surface Magazine, Tuba, Washington Square Review, What Saves Us: Poems of Empathy and Outrage in the Age of Trump,* and *We Are So Happy to Know Something.*

The poems in this book were written between 2005 and 2019. To my friends in Puerto Rico, Boston, New York and elsewhere, my adoptive family of poets, translators, novelists, actors, editors, artists, programmers, musicians, and colleagues, my abiding gratitude for your work and for your instruction, for your continued belief in me and for more than a decade of kindness, patience, and attention.

Ricardo Alberto Maldonado was born and raised in Puerto Rico. He is the co-editor of *Puerto Rico en mi corazón* and the recipient of fellowships from Cantomundo, the New York Foundation for the Arts and Queer|Arts|Mentorship. He lives in New York, where he serves as managing director at 92Y's Unterberg Poetry Center.

Publication of this book was made possible by grants and donations. We are also grateful to those individuals who participated in our 2019 Build a Book Program. They are:

Anonymous (14), Sally Ball, Vincent Bell, Jan Bender-Zanoni, Laurel Blossom, Adam Bohannon, Lee Briccetti, Jane Martha Brox, Anthony Cappo, Carla & Steven Carlson, Andrea Cohen, Janet S. Crossen, Marjorie Deninger, Patrick Donnelly, Charles Douthat, Morgan Driscoll, Lynn Emanuel, Blas Falconer, Monica Ferrell, Joan Fishbein, Jennifer Franklin, Sarah Freligh, Helen Fremont & Donna Thagard, Ryan George, Panio Gianopoulos, Lauri Grossman, Julia Guez, Naomi Guttman & Jonathan Mead, Steven Haas, Bill & Cam Hardy, Lori Hauser, Bill Holgate, Deming Holleran, Piotr Holysz, Nathaniel Hutner, Elizabeth Jackson, Rebecca Kaiser Gibson, Dorothy Tapper Goldman, Voki Kalfayan, David Lee, Howard Levy, Owen Lewis, Jennifer Litt, Sara London & Dean Albarelli, David Long, Ralph & Mary Ann Lowen, Jacquelyn Malone, Fred Marchant, Donna Masini, Louise Mathias, Catherine McArthur, Nathan McClain, Richard McCormick, Kamilah Aisha Moon, James Moore, Beth Morris, John Murillo & Nicole Sealey, Kimberly Nunes, Rebecca Okrent, Jill Pearlman, Marcia & Chris Pelletiere, Maya Pindyck, Megan Pinto, Barbara Preminger, Kevin Prufer, Martha Rhodes, Paula Rhodes, Silvia Rosales, Linda Safyan, Peter & Jill Schireson, Jason Schneiderman, Roni & Richard Schotter, Jane Scovell, Andrew Seligsohn & Martina Anderson, Soraya Shalforoosh, Julie A. Sheehan, James Snyder & Krista Fragos, Alice St. Claire-Long, Megan Staffel, Marjorie & Lew Tesser, Boris Thomas, Pauline Uchmanowicz, Connie Voisine, Martha Webster & Robert Fuentes, Calvin Wei, Bill Wenthe, Allison Benis White, Michelle Whittaker, Rachel Wolff, and Anton Yakovlev.